CONTENTS

FOREWORD

"Creme de la Creme" literally means "cream of the cream" or, translated more freely, "the very best." These pieces were selected both for their beauty (many are time tested favorites) as well as for their appropriateness as classical repertoire for study at a fairly early stage. Many of these have been used traditionally by teachers to provide students with an inviting introduction to the classical repertoire. They all have in common the fact of having very clear patterns; they all tend to focus on a few rather specific musical elements.

They have been organized in the book chronologically rather than by level. In fact, every attempt has been made to keep the level as uniform as possible. Fingerings throughout are provided very sparingly. In most cases they are provided only to indicate changes of position.

© Copyright MCMLXXXVII by Alfred Publishing Co., Inc.

All rights reserved. Printed in USA.

Fanfare

WILLIAM DUNCOMBE

March

JEREMIAH CLARKE

Allegro

Minuet

JEAN-PHILIPPE RAMEAU

Allegretto

Musette

"Gavotte II" from *English Suite No. 3*

JOHANN SEBASTIAN BACH
1685 - 1750

Musette

JOHANN SEBASTIAN BACH

Minuet

LEOPOLD MOZART

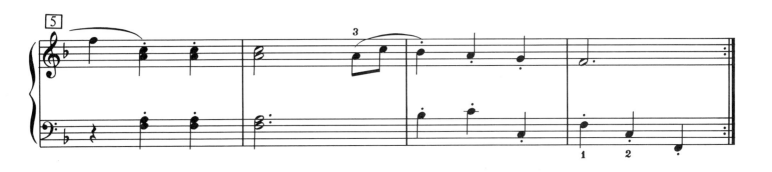

Burleske

LEOPOLD MOZART

L.H. detached throughout

Minuet

LEOPOLD MOZART

Da Capo al Fine

Gypsy Dance

JOSEPH HAYDN

German Dance

JOSEPH HAYDN

Country Dance

JOSEPH HAYDN

Allegretto

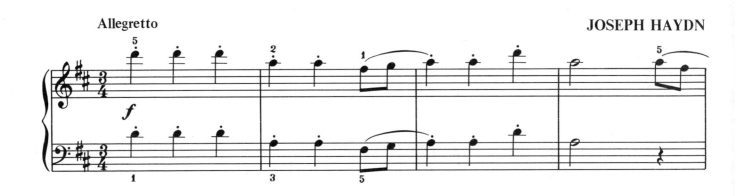

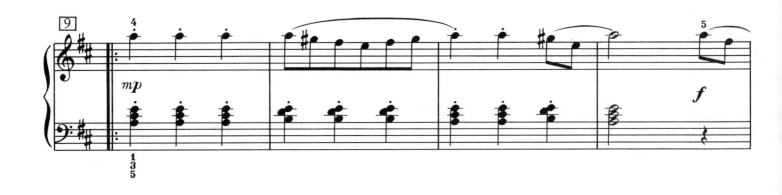

Minuet in C

WOLFGANG AMADEUS MOZART

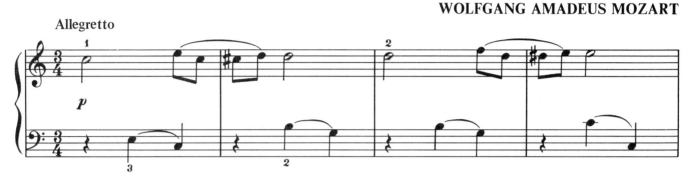

Russian Folk Song I

LUDWIG van BEETHOVEN

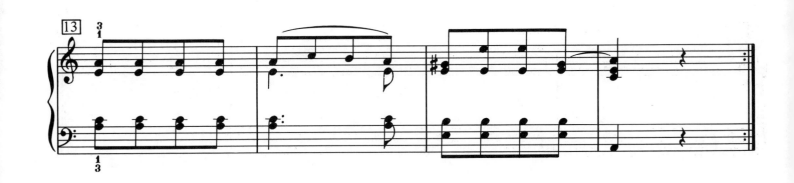

Russian Folk Song II

LUDWIG van BEETHOVEN

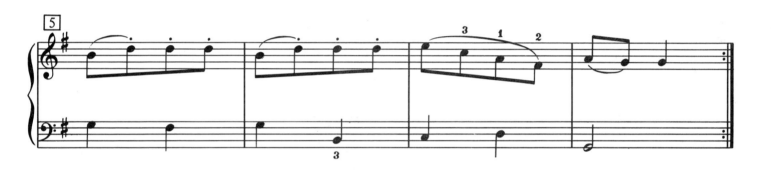

German Dance I

LUDWIG van BEETHOVEN

German Dance II

LUDWIG van BEETHOVEN

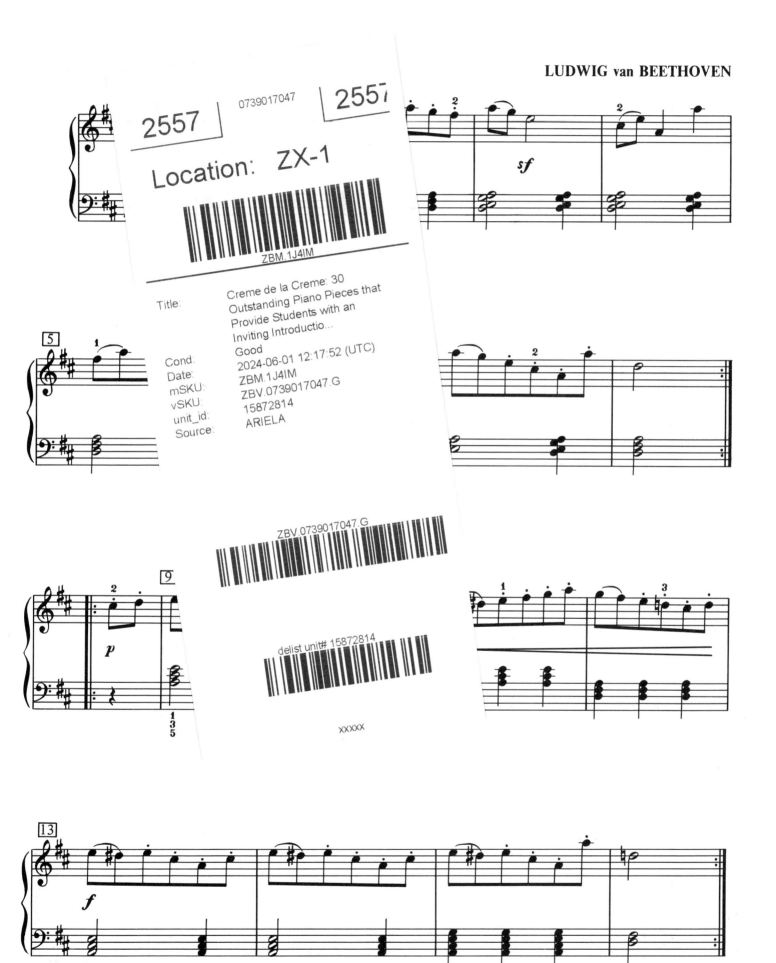

2557 0739017047 2557

Location: ZX-1

ZBM.1J4IM

Title:	Creme de la Creme: 30 Outstanding Piano Pieces that Provide Students with an Inviting Introductio...
Cond:	Good
Date:	2024-06-01 12:17:52 (UTC)
mSKU:	ZBM.1J4IM
vSKU:	ZBV.0739017047.G
unit_id:	15872814
Source:	ARIELA

ZBV.0739017047.G

delist unit# 15872814

xxxxx

Ecossaise

LUDWIG van BEETHOVEN

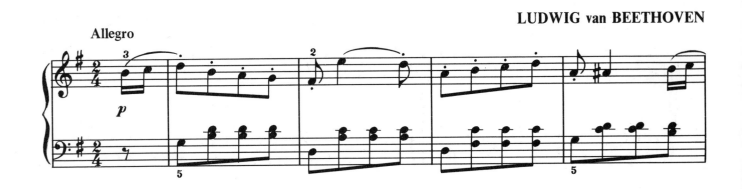

Allegretto

ANTON DIABELLI

Bagatelle

ANTON DIABELLI

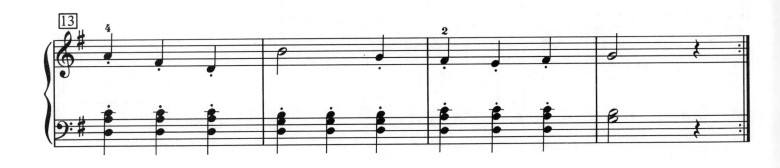

L'Arabesque

JOHANN FRIEDRICH BURGMÜLLER

Restlessness

JOHANN FRIEDRICH BURGMÜLLER

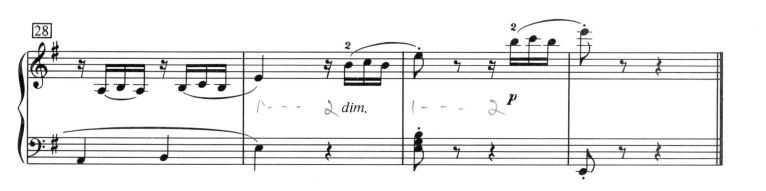

Soldier's March
(Soldatenmarsch)
from Album for the Young

ROBERT SCHUMANN

Playing Soldiers

VLADIMIR REBIKOFF

Folk Song

BÉLA BARTÓK

The Vagabond

BÉLA BARTÓK

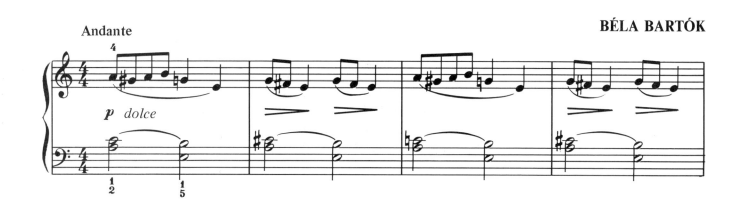

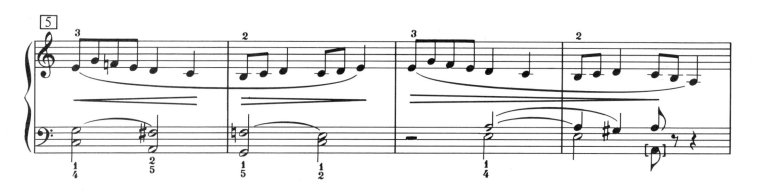

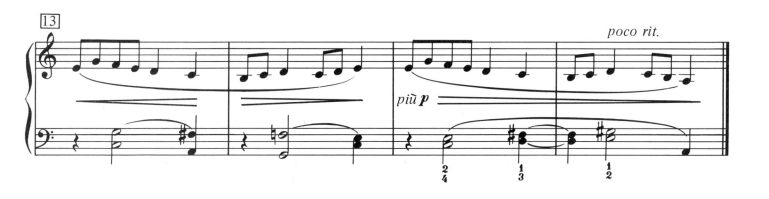

Minuet

No. II from *First Term at the Piano*

BÉLA BARTÓK

Andantino

IGOR STRAVINSKY

Scherzo

from *24 Pieces for Children*

DMITRI KABALEVSKY

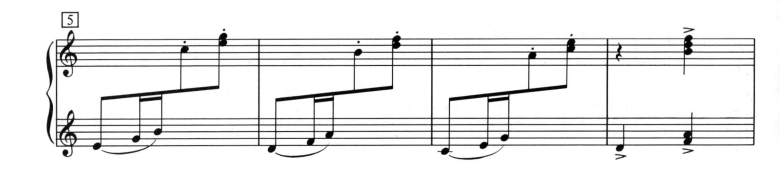

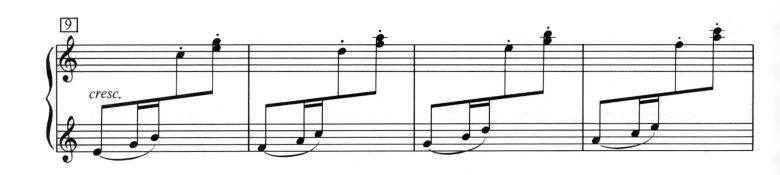

A Little Joke

from *24 Pieces for Children*

DMITRI KABALEVSKY

March

Allegretto

DMITRI SHOSTAKOVICH